Linda —
Thanks fo.
great pu...
and friend!
LORI

Taking your SEAT at the table

Being a Strategic Executive creating Actionable plans and embracing Technology

ISBN-13: 978-1511761420

ISBN-10: 1511761423

HR Topics Publishing
Ft, Myers, FL

lori@hrtopics.com

www.hrtopics.com

Printed in the United States of America

Table of Contents

Introduction

As you may know, my first book was titled "Fire HR Now: Working with HR to shape up or ship out." I am often asked – why would an HR professional write a book encouraging CEOs to fire HR people? The goal of that book is not really to eliminate HR departments or fire people. It is to help CEOs understand why HR is such a critical function and why their management team is not complete until it includes Human Resources as an active member of the leadership team. Each chapter includes a section for the HR professional giving them the tools to work with the CEO on an executive level. At the same time, the book encourages HR professionals to consider whether their current position is right for them. Many HR professionals are stuck in the minutia of administration and don't know how to get out. Fire HR Now! is intended to motivate HR professionals to take their careers to the next level.

I was encouraged to use that title by a number of business leaders and marketing professionals. Yes, the title is provocative – but what HR person is really going to embrace it? I was actually stopped by the manager of the SHRM bookstore at a recent conference who said "Hey, how's that book working out for you?" On reflection, I understood how the title might not be as inclusive as I would have hoped.

If you know that you want to be a contributing leader in your organization, this is the book is for you. It is geared toward HR professionals who want to move their careers to the next level and are looking for a roadmap to follow. We will explore what CEOs want from HR and how you can get there. At the same time, we'll ask you to consider whether your current organization is ready to see you as an executive and options you might have if they are not. This book will help you evaluate your current skill set and future career aspirations. My goal for all Human Resources professionals is that they find meaningful work in organizations that will allow for experiences which provide a more challenging and thoughtful career. HR professionals need to take the reins of their own careers and make great things happen.

Your career may be focused on administration and employee service. If that is where you want your HR career to be, there is no judgment, but this book is not for you. This book is for the HR professional who wants to take their department and career to the next level. This book is geared toward identifying areas the CEO and executive suite are focused on and how you can align your career with those leaders. You may not be ready for the C-suite, but the tips and tools provided in this book will help you take your career to the next level. For those ready to enter the C-suite, we offer insight into the CEO mindset to help you get the Chief Human Resources or Vice President of Human Resources role.

I look forward to walking the journey with you!

Chapter 1

Getting aligned with your CEO

> **"Start with good people, lay out the rules, communicate with your employees, motivate them and reward them. If you do all those things effectively, you can't miss."**

Lee Iacocca, President, CEO and Chairman Chrysler Corporation

Mr. Iacocca shares an enlightened view that is clearly aligned with the idea that an organization needs people to meet their strategic goals. This is a common feeling today among top CEOs. Business has evolved, and organizations have to keep pace. This quote highlights the fact that ultimately HR is the critical function to meet the needs of employees and therefore meet the strategic goals of your organization.

Human Resources is an expensive department for an organization to absorb. While we know the value HR can add, most executives still do not. Executives often still hold the misconception that all

HR does is push paper, enforce policies, and remind them of all the laws that exist to keep managers from implementing plans. They see human resources as the clerk who process benefits and ensures payroll is run on time. If we want to control the destiny of our profession, then we have to take on the role of being our own cheerleader. We can accomplish this by showing the executive team that we are an essential part of the organization's management team.

Competencies in Human Resources

When studying the recent literature on CEOs' concerns as they relate to the human capital in their organizations, we see common threads. The list below is a compilation of the new areas of focus for HR that are common in literature, as well as those that we hear informally from top HR executives. Essentially, the role of HR in the 21st century should be focused on:

- Leadership skills

- Change management

- Succession planning

- Finding and retaining top talent

- Diversity communication

- Analysis and forecasting

Studies found in business literature continue to indicate that CEOs are not interested in HR departments who see their primary focus as day-to-day administration of employee needs. Rather they want to see a focus on how HR can support teams to move strategic organizational goals forward. CEOs are aware of the high level of administration and paperwork in the HR function, but see that as a function of all departments. As a leader, it is your job to get that done behind the scenes and focus your resources on the business.

When was the last time you attended a management meeting and heard accounting talk about cutting checks, or operations talking about putting inventory away on the right shelf? They just do those things. They come to the CEO to discuss a new way to increase speed of receivables, or the return on investment they will attain with a new piece of equipment. No one wants to hear that you're having a hard time finding good people because we don't pay enough - rather go to the table and talk about the common threads in the best new hires of the last six months - and how you plan to attract more of the same.

Your CEO is looking at big picture issues and expects your focus to be on meeting the goals of the strategic plan. There is an expectation in organizations today that the HR leader will be strategic and innovative. Are the conversations you and your CEO having focused on growth and strategy? If your conversations more typically focus on the number of manual checks cut from the payroll run, or the increase in workers compensation claims at any given time you have to shift the focus. Explain to your CEO that you have those things under control, and you want to focus on the issues that will drive strategic initiatives for the organization.

Then come to the table with ideas and solutions that address the strategic needs of your leadership team.

Each CEO and their organization has a unique view of HR. If you do not see your career moving in a direction that embraces the competencies above, you have to evaluate whether you are being forced into a position that is administrative and compliance-oriented in nature. Maybe this is where your CEO and leadership team want you to stay, but if it's not what you want for your career, consider the ways you can take action to drive your career in the right direction.

Career options in Human Resources

Recent work of David Ulrich of the Ross School of Business at the University of Michigan identifies the 20-60-20 formula within the human resources profession. According to Ulrich and his team, 20 percent of HR professionals are currently contributing to business success, 60 percent are making progress toward getting into the top by learning the business and making strategic contributions, and the remaining are either at an entry level or not interested in engaging at the new level of strategic HR. Give thought to where you are and where you want to be. The first step is understanding yourself in an honest way. Only then can you take responsibility for your own career and put actions in place to be in control of your own career.

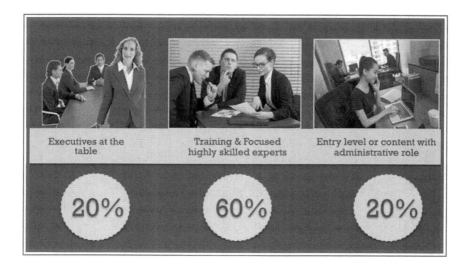

Consider the three career levels in the study. In the chart below, indicate where you feel you are today and where you anticipate your role heading. All levels are important pieces of the HR career puzzle. The question is whether or not your current role – and future aspirations - align with your personal goals. There is no judgment, many professionals choose to stay in support roles to provide a level of work life balance that it is appropriate for their current obligations. This may change for you in the future, and it may not. All we ask now is that you be honest about where you are today and where you want to be in the next 2-3 years. Beyond that – it is hard for any of us to know where life will lead!

	Level of responsibility in Human Resources	Where you are today	Where you would like to your career to be in the next 2-3 years
	Leadership		
	Making Progress; Functional Specialist		
	Entry level or Administrative		

If your columns are aligned – you're in great shape! Throughout the book we will share additional tips and tricks to help you maintain your connections with leadership. If you are not yet where you want to be, we'll give you action-oriented steps you can take to achieve the career of your dreams!

What's your leader thinking

Once you understand your alignment, the next step is to ensure that your CEO or manager is supportive of your vision. Don't guess what your CEO is thinking, go over the chart and explain your thoughts. Ask for confirmation of your selected categories and ask if there is agreement. If so, you are on your way to the next steps in your career. Create a plan with your CEO of meaningful next steps and be accountable to meet the agreed upon goals. However, if your CEO isn't aligned with your goals, now may be the time to evaluate whether your organization can provide the path you have for your career. If there is a question of alignment – now may be the time to read my first book – Fire HR Now! and consider a copy for your boss as well!

The constant improvement in technology requires us to plan for a world in which fewer HR administrators will be needed to do transactional work. We must embrace technology and utilize the functionality of employee and manager self-service if we hope to get out of the administrative functions of human resources. Organizations will expect to have HR professionals who are working on the structure of the organization, providing strategic initiatives, acting as stewards for change, and protecting the corporate culture. HR will always be charged with the execution of the employee needs, but the senior members of the leadership team will expect you to be focused on business issues first.

Do you love taking charge of compliance for your organization? Many HR people do. The HR world is filled with notifications of the latest lawsuit that put a company out of business or the government audit that took days away from critical tasks. But we have to use the compliance responsibility we have to help managers accomplish what they need inside the boundaries of the law. HR compliance is filled with shades of gray and you have to understand how your organization chooses to walk the fine line of being in compliance and still getting its work done. Risk management is a critical function of your role as an HR leader.

Align with your CEO to be sure you are both on the same page of risk tolerance. Organizations tend to vary how they approach risk. Be sure you understand where your CEO is on the spectrum of risk and that you are comfortable advising others in the organization in the same way. A common complaint of management is that HR is a roadblock to everything. To be successful and move up the organizational ladder, you will typically need to be the HR person who advises and educates, but, unless the risk is immanently threatening to the organization, gets out of the manager's way. In other words, pick your battles. If you constantly stand in the way of managers' meeting their needs, you are sure to find yourself out of most decision-making meetings.

Consider the common practice of harassment training, for example. Yes, we all know that it's best practice to train employees annually. But your management team may push back, saying they don't have enough time to take everyone out of production for the same old message. Can you be creative and distribute a policy to stretch the training to every 18 months? Is it possible to have an abbreviated message communicated during open enrollment that all employees will hear? Remember to be the businessperson first. Figure out how to meet your compliance obligations in a way that will keep your company out of court. It is your job to meet the corporate goals and honor legal obligations at the same time.

When speaking with CEOs, we often hear comments regarding HR along the lines of:

"HR departments cost money and they spend the day telling managers what they can't do."

"HR is responsible for the necessary evils of business."

"We'd all be happy if HR just stayed in their office and kept employees from complaining all day."

"What is this nonsense about wanting a seat at the table? There is no table: the management team directs, accounting pays bills, operations produces products, and marketing sells them. Why can't HR simply recruit, manage benefits and run payroll?"

If any of these statements are reflective of your CEO, consider how you are going to create a change of attitude! In order to take your career in the direction of leadership, you need to work for a CEO who deserves, and expects, an HR team that is transformative, innovative, and empowering. You have the opportunity to add value to the top and bottom lines of the operation on a daily basis. If you don't see your CEO and/or leadership team as allowing this to happen, and that's the path you see for yourself, it is up to you to create change or evaluate your options for other career opportunities.

You have options

The tools provided in this book will help you understand and travel your path to leadership. You will consider tips provided to help you start the conversation with your CEO about how you can add value and move into a leadership role. As HR professionals we have to own the administrative tasks, but our future lies in embracing the needs of our organizations for the future.

There are a number of HR professionals who selected the field because they wanted to be in a position to help people, yet we rarely see employee needs making it to the list of CEO concerns. It's not that the CEO doesn't care about their employees. The CEO today assumes that the HR team will handle the employee needs while adding value to the organization. As leaders, we can still connect with our employees and provide high levels of customer service, as long as we understand that the value added in human resources comes from being strategically aligned with the management team.

As the HR executive for your organization, you must appreciate that business is a series of risk-reward decisions. Business functions that impact the organizational bottom-line, like human resources, must have a seat at the decision-making table. As a leader, your job will be to understand the business logic behind the decisions and skillfully be able to communicate them to the rest of the team. You may not agree with all the decisions that are being made, but as a member of the leadership team there will be times you have to put aside your HR hat to be part of a united front. Being part of the conversation allows you to do that with confidence.

Taking your SEAT at the table

Just because you aren't being invited to the table doesn't mean you don't belong there! Human Resources departments have an enormous impact on the bottom line. If you are not invited, take the initiative to point it out to the rest of the management team and make your expectation of participation known. Articles, publications, and research consistently cite corporate budgets that average 55% of line items that impact employees and employee related expenses. While this number varies within each organization, the fact remains that HR will oversee programs and processes that control a significant percentage of your organizational expenditures. That puts you, as the HR leader, on the line to make critical decisions that impact the business on a daily basis. In order to serve your organizational needs, you must have a seat at the decision-making table to ensure alignment in the decisions you make with the strategic plans of the organization.

If you don't immediately see the impact you have on a daily basis, consider the chart below. Outlined are typical areas of a corporate budget and the impact we see HR having on an organization. Your organization will vary – but the impact will generally include these line items at a minimum. If the conversation around these budgetary expenses is occurring without your input, you are missing an opportunity to drive your career, and HR value within the organization, forward.

There will be many areas of the chart that reflect your areas of organizational responsibility. The items in the chart are the topics you should be using to approach "the table." HR professionals tend to talk in terms of people, including what and how a new policy or program will make for a better work environment. We need to talk like business people, in terms of Return On Investment (ROI) and how the top (sales dollars) or bottom line (profits) will be impacted if we take desired actions. Don't talk to executives about the Fair Labor Standards Act, Family and Medical Leave, time-to-hire, etc.; they just don't care. Instead, let them know you are aware of a large incoming production order. In response, you have forecasted the labor demand with an analysis of overtime pay versus use of a temporary labor firm to create additional production hours. Show that you have reviewed this with the operations team and they agree that the issue can be solved with a solution where the

BUDGET LINE ITEM	HR IMPACT
Revenue	▪ Hire top sales talent ▪ Retention of top sales people ▪ Provide training opportunities to support product needs
Labor Cost	▪ Understand and minimize overtime ▪ Recommend additional hires ▪ Cross-training
Unemployment	▪ Proper documentation to support claims ▪ Separate employees when in the interest of business unit ▪ Train of managers on real impact of unemployment
Workers compensation	▪ Safety training and committee ▪ Manage claims ▪ Aggressively assist with return to work
Benefits	▪ Understand benefits that attract and retain employees ▪ Provide work-life balance benefits that are aligned with employee needs ▪ Contribution strategy management ▪ Administrative functionality ▪ Ensure transparency with payroll to eliminate redundancy
Payroll	▪ Self service to eliminate administrative HR activities ▪ Constant review of cost of payroll ▪ Streamline activities to eliminate unnecessary functions

financial impact is still within budget. This is what your CEO is going to care about, and this is how you can elevate yourself to a seat at the leadership table.

Money is the language of business

 If you are not comfortable with business conversations, get yourself training now. There are excellent one day courses in "Finance for non-financial managers" and shortened mini-MBA programs to give you an overall sense of business if you do not have a formal business education. Spend time with finance, marketing and operation counterparts and don't be afraid to ask questions. The most relevant aspects of the business can be learned in informal education at your own organization.

Start all of your conversations with a focus on management decisions and how your solution will ease the challenges they face. For instance, when determining whether to use temporary employees in manufacturing, don't explain the ease of hiring and evaluation of how the candidate fits into the production team. Instead, talk about the ability to manage overtime, have a just-in-time workforce, eliminate cost of hiring, reduction in unemployment rate etc. When you approach executives with data and an anticipated ROI, they will listen. Most importantly, show them you will be accountable for the success of the new project you recommend and report back on the initiative. Your final analysis should include what went well and what you might change the next time you are tasked with a major business initiative.

Most organizations today exist to make money in difficult economic times. Even in the non-profit world, the focus is on generating enough capital to meet the operating demands of the organization in addition to their broader mission. Organizations do not exist for the purpose of making employees happy. All leaders of an organization are expected to understand and support annual revenue-generating and expense goals. HR's mission should be crafted to ensure they have the same focus on profitability and adding value as all other parts of the organization.

Focus on what's keeping management up at night

Business literature continues to refer to the key issues that keep CEOs up at night as:

- Retention of top talent

- Compliance with government regulations

- Availability of mission critical skill sets

Do these issues speak to your CEO's concerns? You need to see the issues that management sees, both internal and external, and create workable initiatives to keep your organization ahead of the curve. Most importantly, you should be approaching your CEO and management team with solutions before they come to you with concerns. Show that you are the leader who knows what needs to be fixed before its broken, and you will be the valuable leadership asset you want to be.

Building your HR function

In the 1990s, Drs. Robert Kaplan and David Norton published the book, "The Balanced Scorecard" as a strategic management concept for business. In it they proposed that all functions of an organization must have goals that are aligned with the strategic plan to ensure an organization's success. We can embrace this in HR by creating programs that drive business innovation and move the administrative function to the lowest possible level, utilizing technology and outsourcing where appropriate. We must partner with the other executives in our organizations to understand the mission of their function. HR should support them through business-oriented programs that remove barriers involving the employee populations. Most importantly, we must be our own champions and use the concept of the balanced scorecard to reinforce our value and alignment of human capital management to the leadership team.

There is no "right way" to build your HR function; it must fit within the culture and structure of your organization. You need to explore the advantages of being an engaged Human Resources executive and create the right team for your organization. This will allow you to shine as a critical and vibrant executive. You may be fortunate enough to have a budget for support personnel. Hire the best and brightest that will support your programs and define a top-performing department for the organization. In smaller organizations, this may be accomplished by relying on vendors to support your administrative needs. Whatever HR structure you choose, build a team around you who puts organizational goals and culture first.

Without the support of your CEO, you will be up a creek without the proverbial paddle if you are striving to be seen in a more visible and strategic role. It is your responsibility to get the leadership team to buy into the concept of engaging human resources as a partner. This can take finesse, but once you accomplish this level of alignment, you will have a career that brings all the challenge and gratification you deserve.

Taking your SEAT at the table

Chapter	2

Setting the stage for leadership

> **There are no secrets to success. It is the result of preparation, hard work, and learning from failure.**

Colin Powell, former United States Secretary of State

The field of human resources closely follows this quote from Colin Powell. HR, as we know it today, began as personnel departments which were very tactical in nature. The primary focus of the personnel department was to meet the needs of the employees so they could quickly return to work. The work ranged from payroll processing and benefit administration to creating policies and gaining an understanding of performance needs. HR also provided administrative services for the organization such as reporting and staffing. In general, the personnel department was seen as an administrative function requiring clerical and customer service skills.

In the 1950s, *Personnel Administrators magazine* had a variety of articles about the need for HR to step up and be heard. The magazine highlighted the idea of getting bosses to listen to thoughts of their personnel administrators and act on new initiatives for the workforce. Many articles highlighted the need to fight for their ideas to be heard or risk nothing being done. Sound familiar? We are still fighting this battle more than 60 years later. We have to champion our own career. CEOs want vocal leaders, and now is your time to shine.

Human Resources today

HR has evolved, but we are still responsible for much of the administrative function historically assigned to human resources. Our goal for HR team members is to focus on the higher level issues that drive the organization forward and add value to the bottom line. Our primary goal in human resources today is to increase alignment with company strategic goals, employee engagement, and productivity, and to assist managers with people focused programs. Meaningful careers can involve leadership in the areas of functional HR needs such as compensation and development. These are generally high-level director and vice-president positions in large organizations. If you have a functional area of HR you embrace, consider the same alignment we discuss in this book with your chief human resources officer and take a seat at the HR leadership table.

HR departments have evolved on many levels and are often considered the shepherds of the culture of their organizations.

Today, executives in high performing organizations rely on HR to communicate critical new business initiatives throughout the organization. Human Resources is often responsible to create the communication, processes, and procedures necessary to ensure that corporate programs are sustainable throughout time.

Our focus is to help you position yourself as a member of the leadership team and get visibility from the executive suite that you deserve. To do this, HR must set out initiatives that will drive the business forward and have meaningful value to the executive team. As shown on the pyramid, we must own and execute all of

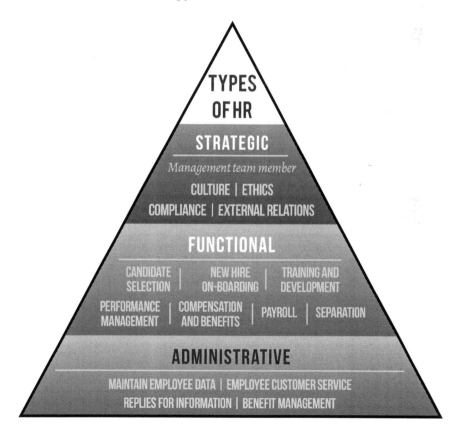

TYPES OF HR

STRATEGIC

Management team member

CULTURE | ETHICS
COMPLIANCE | EXTERNAL RELATIONS

FUNCTIONAL

CANDIDATE SELECTION | NEW HIRE ON-BOARDING | TRAINING AND DEVELOPMENT

PERFORMANCE MANAGEMENT | COMPENSATION AND BENEFITS | PAYROLL | SEPARATION

ADMINISTRATIVE

MAINTAIN EMPLOYEE DATA | EMPLOYEE CUSTOMER SERVICE
REPLIES FOR INFORMATION | BENEFIT MANAGEMENT

the functional and administrative areas of human resources while focusing on strategic programs. HR must insist on an expectation of other managers, executives, and the CEO to trust and respect their input. Empower yourself to be the shepherd of your own career and move forward. Consider your desired career path and contemplate how that can move your career through the levels and needs of the HR function shown in the pyramid.

A challenge of the HR team is to guide employees and other managers through the evolution of the human resources function and where we are today as a profession. Employees know they want help with payroll and benefits. They aren't always concerned about the goals of the HR department. Managers often want you to get their position filled, they don't want to have a conversation concerning the career path available to candidates identified as future top contributors to the organization. Publicize the hierarchy of HR responsibility and insist that others understand your priorities.

How many HR people does it take?

As human resource leaders take on more responsibility associated with the overall business, there will be new people or systems required to handle the day-to-day HR function. It can be difficult to add to the HR headcount, and it's not always necessary. This conversation always begs the question... how many HR people do we really need? The answer to that question will be influenced by the goals of HR for your organization, but there are baseline studies that can be considered for comparison.

The ratio of HR team members to organizational employees remained fairly stable at one HR professional for every 100 employees in the last half of the 20th century. There has been a change as we entered the 21st century. The reduction in HR staff

> SHRM survey - Median is 1:100 Average is 1:145
>
> The HR Scorecard: Linking People, Strategy, and Performance
>
> High Quality HR Leadership - 1:139
>
> Low Quality of HR leadership - 1:253

is noted in a recent SHRM Trend survey, which shows that the average organization has one HR team member for every 145 employees. Additional research from the book The HR Scorecard demonstrates the large difference in ratio that can be found in HR organizations. It is interesting to see the disparity they show between the numbers of HR professionals based on the level of organizational performance. This may be a study worth sharing with your CEO if you are having trouble adding needed members to your HR team!

The reduction in headcount of the HR function can be attributed to both economic necessity and the technological advances that are available to HR teams in organizations of all sizes. As with all benchmark data, these figures are a generalization for all organizations. The ratio that is appropriate for your organization may change based on factors such as:

- ☞ Sophistication of your workforce

- ☞ Number of dispersed locations

- ☞ Company size

- ☞ Cultural alignment with employee service

- ☞ Outsourced activities and services

Averages are just that: the top of the bell curve. You may want a more integrated HR team or prefer one that requires employees to be more self sufficient in meeting their needs around payroll and benefits, for example. Considering the HR Scorecard data, there are options for your team based on the expectations of employee service. Use the tool below to find talking points for a conversation with your CEO and management team to determine the right ratio for your organization.

	Indicate a Number or High Medium Low
Current number of employees	
Number of employees anticipated to join the organization in next 12 months (including replacement for those leaving)	
Level of service to align with organizational culture	
Employees ability/desire to be self sufficient	
Use of temps and/or independent contractors	
Needs of employees outside of main office	
Current use of technology or plan to add technology in the future	
Ability for vendors to support HR (outsourcing)	
Recommendation for number of HR team members based on an average of 1 to 145 employees	

There is no right or wrong number of HR team members, but a ratio of employees to HR team can be evaluated based on these criteria. You and your management team must be comfortable with the size of the human resources department and the level of service to be provided. You should be confident that the HR team can support the needs of the organization without being bogged down in administrative tasks.

Using these data points, you have benchmarks and a forum for discussion for the appropriate size of the HR function in your organization. Use this information to confirm that the leadership team is in agreement with the level of services to be provided based on the size and budget of your HR team. If there is not a budget to add the HR headcount you feel is required, at least you will have had a productive business conversations and be able to set boundaries around expectations.

Who is leading HR?

The title of HR leaders has also evolved over the years. Today, where the goal of HR alignment within business is desired, the HR executive generally holds the title of Chief Human Resources Officer or Vice President of Human Resources. This person reports directly to the CEO. In smaller organizations, the title might be Director of Human Resources or Administrative Manager, and the function may even be part of a larger role, such as Chief Financial Officer or Office Manager. Regardless of the title, we recommend the reporting relationship for the HR function of the position be to the chief executive to ensure alignment with the organizational strategy. The relationship with the CEO is critical. HR employees who report to another manager, such as chief financial officer, will align their goals more closely with their boss'. This generally creates a situation where HR initiatives are not created for the good of the overall organization, but are aligned with the individual goals of the leader to whom they report. Alignment with the CEO sends a message to all employees that HR is to be focused first on the overall goals of the organization and not one particular area.

The HR generalist of the 21st century has evolved to positions that are titled "HR Business Partner" (HRBP) in many organizations. The title is created to emphasize alignment with the operation and removes all responsibility of administrative functions from the HR position. Generally, the HRBP is focused on the strategic areas of the business, utilizing HR functional specialists. Specialist roles typically include Director of Compensation, Recruiting, and Organizational Development to name a few. We find these areas residing in the middle section of our functional pyramid. Organizations with the HRBP function have generally moved benefit administration, payroll, and employee inquiry to a service center model staffed with entry-level employees who answer all questions for the employee population. In small organizations, the HRBP may have an outsourced vendor that provides the administrative functions.

The administration in service center structures rarely has a "personal touch" and often conducts their interactions with employees strictly by email. The service center can be internal or external to an organization, although most large organizations (more than 5,000 employees) utilize an external service provider. Whether the service center is internal to your company or a third party vendor, there will also be a reduced focus on customer service. Employees are expected to handle their administrative needs through self-service portals. This is not necessarily bad. Technology will give employees access to their needs around the clock and will provide employees a level of privacy when dealing with a sensitive HR issue rather than going to a co-worker in the human resources department.

The leaders of HR today have changed in their basic skill sets. The competencies needed from HR business partners and leaders can be discovered in the list below. Review the list with a critical eye and determine if whether you bring these skills to your current role.

- Communicative

- Professional

- Decisive

- Responsive

- Business savvy

- Facilitator

And, most importantly...

➲ Problem Solver

If you don't have the skills today – are you interested in gaining these competencies? How might you go about getting training or development in areas of weakness? Be honest with yourself. Only by embracing these competencies will be you able to move up to the C-suite and find the leadership career you are expecting to have.

Is this what you want?

You should also be sure that you are surrounding yourself with mentors and leaders you trust and respect. Look around at the leadership team in your organization and ask yourself a few questions:

☞ Are these the people whom you consider your peers?

☞ Do you want to elevate your responsibilities to be part of the leadership team?

☞ Is the current team made up of people you feel you can learn from and grow with?

☞ Do you respect this team because of their actions and commitment?

We all have choices in life. You will be spending a great deal of time with the other leaders in your organization. During the workday there will be an expectation that you support one another and are interested in their thoughts. As you assess your personal career goals, leave open the possibility that you have the right skills in the wrong environment!

Leaders need to be focused on business and putting the goals of the business operation ahead of their areas of expertise. When you attend meetings, do the subjects of new equipment, financing and top customer concerns excite you, or do you

"zone out" and start thinking about the company picnic? Are you intrigued to hear about inventory cycles and how purchasing can drive more economical buying patterns? Reflecting on this will help you evaluate whether the position of a business executive representing HR is one that you are even interested in fighting for. You must be interested in knowing the business, asking good questions, and positioning HR as the group that will be a partner to management. Meet the needs of the business and focus strategically on all initiatives that will impact the overall goals for the organization and you will get that invitation to lead. To do so, others must feel confident that your number one focus is to solve business problems.

Today, executives expect that the human resources leader will be aligned with the organizational mission, understand the strategic goals, and work to enact initiatives that will drive these forward. There must be a cultural fit between HR and the rest of the organization and a place for risk/reward conversations to take place. HR must be flexible and adaptable; not locked into the current system and processes. Change management is the new driver in HR when we are called on to guide employees as the organization uncovers new opportunities or threats. As such, we expect HR to use compliance as a guideline for decision-making, not a codebook from which deviation is impossible. Businesses must be nimble and ready to move as the market or other forces require attention. Your HR function should be no different.

Self reflection and evaluation

Use the chart on the next page to accurately assess your current participation in business activities. You will reflect on the items you currently participate in, those you are interested in, and those in which you have no interest. The action items on the chart are expectations of the HR executive and a good way for you to benchmark where your interest lies in the next steps associated with executive-level positions. It will also help you to identify development opportunities for yourself. We challenge HR professionals to consider if an executive role is of interest. If not, a decision should be made to move into a role that is more accurately aligned with your long-term career plans and skill set.

Once you have completed the chart, use the point system below to determine an overall score. This is not an evaluation of a good or bad HR professional, just a way to reflect on the fit with your aspirations and the organizational needs. It will also help uncover areas of training and development that might get you where you want to go.

Getting a **SEAT** at the table

Y= Currently do this activity C = Capable of this; but not participating in this area/activity TN= I would like to do this, but training is needed NI = I am not interested in this activity			
Participate in anual budgeting		Spend time each week with Varoius department team members	
Know the budgeted EBITA and what components are critical for attaining the goal		Has spent portion of career in an area outside HR	
Name 5 customers generating the highest revenue		Serve as trusted advisors for others on leadership team	
Identify top 3 profitable products or services		Communicates legislative changes and compliance issues with a focus applicable to our business	
Name the top three competitors			
What is the top concern or goal of each business are of the organization		Annual goals focused on business rather then HR	
Evaluate strategic action items for future implementation		Provide HR metrics to support business planning	
Know key metrics; evaluate against success on regular basis		Proactive about addressing issues for employees and managers	
Collaborate across business units		HR policies support efficiencies and compliance	
Management team is primary work group		Training is focused on business relevant skills and succession planning	
Present HR budget based on data and ROI			
Facilitate win-win in difficult situations		Influences employee engagement and performance through communication	
Participate in lifelong learning beyond current HR role		Create opportunities for executives, managers and team members to understand and embody the culture the corporation desires	
Compliance situations are presented with logical business ramifications			
Talk about challenges and ask others outside HR for input		Processes are necessary and automated or minimized where possible	
Spend time each week with various department team members		Give yourself 1 point for finishing!	

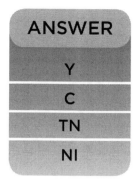
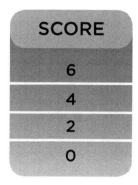

ANSWER	SCORE
Y	6
C	4
TN	2
NI	0

For scores of 134 or above, you are an aligned business partner. Consider opportunities to integrate HR into additional areas of the business. You may also consider ways to ensure that the other members of the HR team are aligned with the same high-level skills and competencies that ensure a succession path for the future.

Scores of 110 through 133 indicate a desire to participate at an executive level. Consider having an open conversation with your CEO about your expectations and strengths of HR within your organization. Discuss with all managers how having a strategic HR function will serve to meet the needs of the organization as a whole. Ask for a budget and a SEAT at the table so that you may gain the experiences to enhance your career.

Scores of 88 through 109 indicate a need for thoughtful consideration of your goals. You might not want to participate at an innovative and strategic level. As long as your CEO and management team agree, this may work for your organization. However, if the leaders are looking for a strategic human resources function, you might consider whether adding a higher-level team member is appropriate. You may also find yourself seeking a role in a larger organization as a subject matter expert. Consider Director of Recruiting, Compensation or Talent for example.

Scores below 88 would indicate your view of HR is focused on outstanding administration and internal customer focused. This may be perfectly appropriate if you are new to the field of HR, or focused on an area of human resources that provides this service for strategically aligned HR partners. If you feel you are stuck here due to your organization constraints, consider additional outsourcing. If this is where you are comfortable, it may work well for you as long as your organization is on the same page.

Taking the next step

With a common base of knowledge as to where HR has been, CEOs' literature on where HR is and where you want your career to go, we are now ready to get you there. The next four chapters will take you through the steps that are necessary to join the leadership team... taking that SEAT at the table!

- ⚐   Strategic alignment and initiatives

- ⚐   Executive level management expectations

- ⚐   Action oriented and accountable HR leaders

- ⚐   Tech-savvy systems to ease the burden

Moving into a leadership role will be one of the most rewarding career steps you can make. It will be hard work, but the skills gained and relationships formed will be worth every late night! Take the journey with us, and you will have the tools you need for success.

Chapter 3

Strategic alignment

> **The biggest risk is not taking any risk... In a world that is changing really quickly, the only strategy that is guaranteed to fail is not taking risks.**

Mark Zukerberg, Founder and CEO Facebook

Strategy is created and meant to be altered – all in the interest of moving the organization forward. Business is a series of risk reward decisions. HR must embrace the change the world hands us and help the organization create plans that will adapt to a new normal at any given time. Strategy is not about providing the perfect solution, but rather a guiding principle that can be followed.

In the broadest sense, HR has always been and will always be about supporting the strategic mission through people. You do that by engaging team members every day with an HR team that understands the components of the business. Working with managers we can ensure that the functional teams have the tools they need to drive the mission. The new link is to understand how tactical functions of HR are being handled while your team is driving the organization in the direction set by the CEO. This is what strategy is all about.

> **"Hell, there are no rules here - we're trying to accomplish something."**

Thomas Edison, American inventor and businessman

HR often waits for the management team to arrive at the realization that we can be helpful and invite us to the leadership table on their own. Your career may not have this much time! Stand up, state your case, and get yourself the strategic invitation today. Do this by showing other managers the value you can bring even before you are invited. This is the first rule you need to break – remember, as Thomas Edison said – we're trying to create something here.

Be vocal and join the team

It is your responsibility to be the voice within your organization that the goal of human resources isn't simply getting people in seats, running payroll, and administering benefits. Those are the tactical pieces that you must ensure are in place before you undertake strategic initiatives, but that is just part of the day's work. Sure, your HR department can be strictly administrative, but we want to argue that the risk of that is great, and the rewards they forego are plentiful. Instead, provide the same business-minded excellence you see from your other strategic functions and insist that your leadership team use human resources as a competitive advantage to meet organizational goals.

> **A bird doesn't sign because it has an answer, it sings because it has a song**

Joan Walsh Anglund

If you are part of the strategic planning process today, be sure your top goals for the year are aligned to meet the overall strategic plan. If you are not part of the team, or your organization does not have formal strategic planning, make an appointment with the CEO and find out what the top initiatives are. Then set goals for yourself that will support the organization in meeting those goals. Make it clear to your team and other managers that your focus is strategic excellence, and you plan to participate whether invited or not.

Aligning human capital with strategy

At the very core, how your organization incorporates human capital and the human resources function is the first strategic analysis to provide leadership. Specifically, how can your organization utilize HR to drive their mission and strategic plans forward? HR will add strategic value by understanding the sales and production requirements that ensure you have the talent and bench strength to meet the future goals of your organization. Knowing where your organization is compared to budget on a regular basis will help you make decisions relating to vendor selection and staffing plans, which will impact the overall financial health of the organization.

At a recent training session of HR professionals in Chicago, the top issues discussed were common topics that we have struggled with for years. The interesting twist is that we saw a slant toward integrating these issues into the overall organizational strategy. The top HR leaders at the meeting wanted to talk about how to link HR activity with impact to the bottom line. The critical issues the HR executives asked the group to address at this meeting were:

- Defining career progression so that the organization is able to attract and retain the best and brightest

- Transforming HR responsibility so that the department is linked to tangible business results

- Ensuring that employee training and development lives beyond the classroom

- Cultural integration during mergers and acquisition

Human Resources has not left the traditional focus of recruiting, training, and company culture out of our programs. However, we are starting to see an expansion on the traditional. We see a desire for collaboration around a big-picture view of human resources that is required by our organization. Leaders are no longer focused on recruiting as a "fill the seat" activity. They are focusing on how recruiting can create long-term career paths for succession planning and ensure employee engagement for long-term retention.

Talk the language of business

Work with your CEO to set strategic initiatives that meet leadership needs and ensure alignment with the organization as well as forwarding your own career aspirations. Create measurable goals for human resources that are meaningful within the context of goals for the organization. Understand the constraints of your organization, and be certain that the timeline you set is realistic. Work with your CEO to generate five to seven meaningful initiatives that will solve the issues keeping them up at night. Yes, all the other work has to be completed as well, but the strategic goals are those that are going to get you into David Ulrich's definition of the top 20 percent of HR professionals (see Chapter 1).

To be part of the strategic team, you need to know the business. The leadership team will not be impressed with your extensive HR knowledge. You will have to stay current on the issues that are relevant to operations, sales, and finance. To do this, you must understand the context in which each functional area exists. Having an understanding of the goals of each of the stakeholders in the business will be critical to your success. Get to know your peers, take board members to lunch, and attend other department meetings just to listen. Understand where the financing comes from and be sure you are aligned with those interests as well. The business strategy must be clear to you if you are to drive its basic tenants throughout the organization. Embrace the business strategy in everything you do.

A primary principal of strategic planning is the SWOT analysis. This looks at the Strengths, Weaknesses, Opportunities, and Threats of an organization. If you were not part of the strategic plan in your organization, take time to talk to your leadership team about what they saw as the key elements in these areas. If you were part of the planning, reflect on the issues that came up during the discussion. Then use the chart below to understand how HR strategy can be developed to support or minimize the effect of each. Share this with your HR team, so they understand the impact they have on strategy every day.

	Organizational view/issue	HR alignment with view or issue; solutions you can recommend
Strengths of Organization		
Weaknesses of Organization		
Opportunities in external environment		
Threats in external environment		

SWOT analysis allows leaders to frame their strategic plan as actions to be taken. Problem solving is a key component to strategic management and a critical skill to embrace as an HR leader. In evaluating the weaknesses and threats, leaders create plans that address these as opportunities – or at least minimize the impact on the organization. As an HR member of the team, you bring the unique perspective of being somewhat of an outsider to the typical business conversation while still having an inside knowledge of the organizational operations and culture. You can use this position to challenge the leadership team when they fall back into the routine of "that's how we've always done it" line of planning.

Use your knowledge of the strategic plan to help set initiatives for your HR function that will drive the overall strategic plan forward. When you hear of new equipment being purchased in manufacturing, set a meeting with the vendor to understand the skills needed for production staff. Investigate training opportunities and create a list of employees currently on the team that have those skills. If new skills are needed, look for government funding to enhance the skills of your employees. You'll be the star of the next management meeting when you arrive with this critical information long before they thought to ask for it.

Embrace new ideas

Be strategic in your implementation of resources and new work arrangements. The diversity in the way work is accomplished today adds complexity to the job of the human resources department. Managing these relationships takes time and skills that need to be acquired. According to a Deloitte study entitled "Human Capital Trends 2013," we are in an "open talent economy – a collaborative, transparent, technology-driven, rapid-cycle way of doing business." Contractors, part-time workers, and tele-commuters are all viable options available in the workforce.

Outsourcing has become an increasingly popular alternative for many organizations. While outsourcing is generally seen as a way to reduce headcount, HR professionals should frame strategic outsourcing as a way to bring top talent and skills into the organization where expertise does not exist.

There are strategic business reasons to embrace these new ways of work as a way of eliminating various burdens and expenses to the organization. Consider each of these opportunities as you look at the SWOT analysis and the assessment of the employee population. The flexibility and diversity of work should be evaluated against the goals of the organization to determine where they make sense and where they just won't work. Consider bringing the concept to the leadership team with a focus on attainment of goals and the return on investment they will provide. Even if your analysis determines the processes are not feasible, discuss the thoughts with the leadership team to highlight the fact that you reviewed strategic opportunities and ask for feedback if they feel anything has been missed. This demonstrates your strategic focus as well as the desire to collaborate with the rest of the team.

As an HR executive, you must focus on the drivers of your business, including cost factors, competitors, service, and technology. HR needs to understand the barriers to success and be aligned with strategy to address these issues. This is critical in all areas of the employee life cycle. When evaluating aspects such as pay policy, training programs, and how to recruit, you have to make decisions that are grounded in the best interest of the long-term success of your organization. This should be in alignment with the short- and long-term goals of the overall organization – not just what makes sense for HR.

> Be a STRATEGIC partner to your leadership team as your first step to taking that SEAT at the table.

Taking your SEAT at the table

Chapter 4

Executive leadership

> **Learn from yesterday, live for today, hope for tomorrow.**
>
> **The important thing is not to stop questioning.**

Albert Einstein, Inventor

You may have the top HR title today; you may even sit on the management team. But being an executive is a great deal more than just being at the top of the food chain. Executives are those that are leaders – and in leading, allow others to grow and be successful as well. The next few pages will lay out skills consistently found among top executives. Be reflective about your own skillset and interactions. An awareness of yourself and your actions will help you determine which executive level skills you may need to embrace or develop.

It takes work

Moving into an executive role is a lot of work. If you are reading this book as an HR professional, we will assume you know human resources. You can answer most HR questions in your sleep. You likely arrive at work with a plan for the day – and find that is quickly derailed by employee needs! You have your HR team, or at least vendors, and know what is expected of human resources in your organization.

But business doesn't run with fences around each department. Executives in organizations must interact and collaborate all day to ensure pieces of the puzzle continue to fit into one cohesive  picture. Having a seat at the table will require you to see the whole organizational picture and ensure that your contributions are harmonious with the greater goal. As an executive, you need to plan your day with other departments in mind.

If you are forging a place in your organization where human resources will be considered an executive role, embrace the fact that this will take energy, consensus-building, and sleepless nights. You may have to return to school to brush up on accounting or marketing. Sounds like a lot of work - so why bother?

Being an executive is interesting and challenging. Moving your human resources career from a tactical to an executive level partner will provide the long-term success of human resources in your organization. You will be meeting the real needs of the business, not just checking tasks off a list. You will be seen as a leader who solves business problems and can be counted on to provide valuable insight to mission-critical initiatives. And...you will be learning new things and engaging with people that bring fresh perspective to your HR function. This can be empowering and validating as your career progresses.

New competencies to embrace

The University of Michigan team presented a Human Resource Competency Study in 2013 that identifies six critical competencies seen in the human resources leaders of today. According to this study, competencies a human resources professional will need to include in their skill set are:

- Credible Activist

- Strategically Positioned

- Capability Builder

- Change Champion

- Integrator and Innovator

- Technology Proponent

These words work together to paint a picture of an executive who can understand the business first and implement HR actions that will align with the whole organization. They demonstrate a role that is excited and engaged with the operations of the business. These are your new building blocks of the 21st century as an HR executive. You must embrace them or be prepared to get out of the way of the leadership team.

HR executives must be reflective of the organizational culture and be able to speak fluently about the business operation. You should be approachable to all internally, but as an executive, be able to separate yourself from the employee population. You must know and understand "the gang" without being a member of the group. Your writing skills should provide a level of communication that demonstrates executive experience while still being in touch with the internal culture. Communication skills and flexibility should be top competencies to master and are utilized daily in both formal and informal interactions. On a daily basis you need to be able to use the language of the executive suite, but at the same time speak with respect to employees for whom English may not be their first language. You should frequently spend time in the break room asking employees about their family and needs while still presenting yourself as a leader. This can be a difficult balancing act for some but one worth working toward to fulfill your HR career aspirations.

Being a business executive may mean being on the front lines of the operation and thinking like an entrepreneur. As you reflect upon the business in which you work, what do you identify that could be done differently? As the HR department, you typically aren't as involved in daily operations, cash flow, and customer relations.

So, when others are faced with challenges you can be a business resource able to provide out-of-the-box suggestions. Be the one member of management who can see past the trees to the forest. Being on the outside looking in can be exactly the type of advocate your executive team is looking for.

> **"Say yes and we'll figure it out afterward"**

Tina Fey, actress

Are you a devil's advocate for the decisions being considered or do you just go along with the group for fear of rocking the boat? Madeline Albright, the first female Secretary of State, was quoted as saying that she often held her tongue in cabinet meetings for fear she didn't have the right thought, only to find another cabinet member make the exact point a few minutes later. Be analytical of situations in the organization, speak-up and push back respectfully when you see the team moving toward decisions that are reflective of the past or that you do not consider unique solutions.

Be seen and heard

You will have to carve time out of your day for other executives in other business units that want to discuss topics of importance to their function. Fellow executives may want time to further discuss a point you made at the last meeting. This may seem impossible with what is currently on your plate, but it's a key component of being an executive first. It is crucial that you understand each functional area and the challenges faced by their team.

You should attend other departmental meetings on a regular basis not to talk about human resources, but to listen and learn about the successes and failures of other functional areas. Don't wait to be invited – let the meeting organizer know that you are interested in their issues and you will be attending as a confidential observer. This is how you will build high-level relationships across the organization and create the constituency of other leaders, which will help move your initiatives forward. That's what being an executive is all about.

Executives step outside their box and are a visible presence in the organization. Don't allow yourself to be restricted by your HR title. Be seen throughout the organization as a leader who puts the team first. Ensure that all employees understand you are focused on the success of the company as your first concern. When you attend meetings sit in the middle of the action...or even at the head of the table! Be sure the leadership meetings have a place on the agenda for at least one item impacting human resources. Then be prepared to deliver information in a concise and data driven presentation. Don't focus on the HR implications; focus on the impact for the overall business.

An added bonus you will bring to the executive team is your unique perspective to management meetings. HR will typically hear things through the grapevine that provide a different slant than what your fellow executives are hearing. They may miss the far reaching impact of a decision while they are focused on their functional areas, but as HR you interact with everyone. You can be the "inside outsider" in these meetings that challenges assumptions and digs deeper into situations others may see as routine. Often, this opens leaders up to question traditional assumptions or causes them to consider a new viewpoint, which leads to operational excellence.

Participating at an executive level with other managers will lead to initiatives in recruiting, training, and rewards that drive meaningful results to the business. These will no longer be actions to be completed; they will be strategic components of the business that all managers understand are necessary to achieve the goals established by leadership.

Create strong relationships

Communication and patience are critical competencies organizations expect to see on a daily basis from HR. The HR department has many internal and external constituents they need to manage on a daily basis. Working with line employees, executives, and the external community simultaneously, the key is to be a flexible yet decisive executive who is clearly at the helm of the HR ship. You must be able to professionally represent your organization to external organizations in addition to your internal role. Viewing your position as an executive first, you must understand that you are the representative of your organization to the public in many situations.

You likely started your HR career in an entry-level, administrative function. Then you were promoted, not because you entered the benefits enrollment the fastest, but because someone saw competencies in you that were valued in the organization. You may have been in another area of the company and someone asked you to fill a vacancy in HR. Typically, the traits you possess which attracted this attention include strategic thinking, teamwork, ethical behavior, creating opportunities, communication, and problem solving. These are the traits that align with the top-notch HR executive your CEO is looking for. Be your own advocate and highlight these skills in the projects you choose to move forward. Doing this will bring attention to your leadership style and allow you to achieve your full potential.

You are a business person first

You will still spend time considering employee concerns, but now you will put an emphasis on how the issue fits into the overall operation. You need to be able to listen, coach, and advise in a way that is best for the organization, not necessarily the employee. HR must understand we are a part of a leadership team that understands and puts the mission of the organization first. It is our responsibility to align employee expectations with the realistic possibilities that exist in your organization. That often means we are at odds with employee demands and must participate in and enforce difficult decisions.

If you have not had formal business training, consider earning an MBA or attending another business-focused program. At this point in your career, you can gain HR knowledge through seminars, conferences, and certifications, but these should not be the focus of your development. Business knowledge is a critical part of your ongoing education, and now is the time to focus on it. There are many shorter programs intended to get those who have not been in traditional business programs up to speed quickly. Options may include mini-MBA programs, exposure to online coursework, community leadership training, and certificate programs through universities. Whatever path you choose, be sure you have the vocabulary and business acumen to be able to participate at the executive level. These steps take time and energy, but the payoff is a well-rounded businessperson possessing a myriad of options for future career growth.

HR is charged with the responsibility of employee communication in most organizations. However, if HR does not participate at an executive level in the decision-making, the foundation behind the change is missing. This makes it difficult to communicate with employees about a new decision. Typical decisions are made over the course of many management meetings reviewing data and looking a variety of options for change. It may be difficult to communicate to employees why there is not a company picnic this year if you weren't present to establish the budget and understand the need to cut the expense. If you participated in the annual budget planning you would have a better understanding of why the change was required. Or...maybe you're not even given a budget! Help the leadership team understand that by including you in these executive conversations, you will have a basis for understanding the financial constraints of the organization and can better communicate that to the employee population.

Get involved outside your organization

Participating outside the organization is a critical aspect of being an executive. A skilled HR executive will increase exposure to the business and its customers as well as gain critical depth of knowledge to bring back to the HR team. This will take resources, both time and money, but will pay off tremendously in the base of knowledge brought to the HR function going forward.

There are many options for executive level interaction including:

- Mastermind groups

- Vendor user groups

- Non-profit board

- Industry association involvement

Most executives find a way to connect with those outside the organization, and the HR leader should do the same. At a minimum, you should attend industry conferences, represent your organization on professional committees, and participate in the local community. Volunteer work at the non-profit of your choice, for example, is a great way to connect with others in the community and to learn how other organizations make decisions and develop policies and programs. Mastermind groups are a form of peer-to-peer advisory groups which are becoming more available for those in HR, and these are a great way to make connections and share tips and tricks with others who many be facing similar situations.

If you are not familiar with these groups, ask your accountant, lawyer, benefit consultant, or payroll vendor if they know of groups in which you can participate. Outside connections provide a resource you can tap into so that you don't have to reinvent the wheel with each new initiative that you face. Participation with diverse groups will provide opportunities for you to increase your leadership skills as well as gain insight into how other businesses operate.

As a member of the executive team, HR should be a trusted confidant and sounding board to the other internal leaders. Generally we find that HR is the interpersonal expert on the leadership team, and as such you should be available to coach other executives regarding confidential information and situations. At the executive level peers must be able to trust that the HR executive will listen to issues and situations with an open mind and closed lips. This is a critical element of the HR executive in successful organizations.

Fight the right fight

Another critical characteristic of an HR executive is to be adaptable and know which issues are worth fighting for. The foundations of your HR function should be listening, learning, and making decisions. Your HR team must have policies and operate within those policies. But at the same time, you need to make decisions in the best interest of the business environment. An HR manager who points to policies in the handbook for every decision will not be the one invited into the executive suite. Policies must exist, but at times they must also be bent or even broken.

For example, consider an employee who loses an aunt. Under most policies, this would not qualify for bereavement leave. The employee comes to HR to explain that his mother died when he was twelve, and this aunt stepped in and provided emotional support to him for the past twenty-five years. The aunt resides in Florida, and there is no one to arrange a memorial event. Do you really want to be the HR function that quotes the handbook and reminds the employee that no paid time is available for an aunt and that vacation needs to be requested two weeks in advance? Wouldn't it support the culture of your organization for HR to consider the special circumstance, speak with the direct manager (who is now a peer of the HR executive) and make a decision in light of the specific facts of the case?

> **Be an EXECUTIVE partner to your leadership team as your second step to taking that SEAT at the table.**

Chapter	5

Action-oriented and Accountable

> **Just remember, you can do anything you set your mind to, but it takes action, perseverance, and facing your fears.**

Gillian Anderson, Actress

Likely your CEO is not looking for an HR administrator to be a member of the management team. They look for strategic leaders who can take action. Parallel to what Ms. Anderson says, you've got to move, stick with it, and not worry about the downside. There is an expectation that leaders will be accountable for their projects and revise actions when needed. The "A" in our model must stand for action-oriented and accountable ...not administrative if you want a SEAT at the leadership table.

Taking the right action

In any HR department, the administrative tasks need to be completed. Whether you outsource, have an entry-level associate, or count on assistance from others, the work needs to get done. Often you find it is just easier to do it yourself rather than train and rely on someone else to do it as well as you can. But this can't be your solution. The more you allow yourself to get bogged down with administration, the less time you will have for strategic and executive level performance.

Think about what action items you have on your plate for the next ten days. Write down the top three on the space below.

1. _____

2. _____

3. _____

Now consider the strategic implications for your organization. Circle the actions above that support those goals and help the leadership team drive success for the current year. If you are able to circle at least two of the goals, you are in great shape to take a SEAT at the table. If the actions don't support the strategy directly, now is the time to get aligned with the leadership team and create goals that will be meaningful to the organization.

> Don't say you don't have enough time. You have exactly the same number of hours per day that were given to Helen Keller, Michelangelo, Mother Teresa, Thomas Jefferson, and Albert Einstein.

– H Jackson Brown Jr, Author

Review your action items again and consider the impact to the organization. Are the action items internal, HR-facing initiatives such as completing FMLA forms, updating employee files, and filling an open position? If so, consider whether you are positioning yourself as an executive. The ideal action items should contain elements that reflect organizational business goals and initiatives that meet the needs of key stakeholders. You can accomplish this by targeting programs within the scope of HR but focused on the overall business, not the HR department. For example, evaluating a new biometric time clock to minimize overtime paid (not to mention buddy punching!) or implementing a new training program so additional employees are able to utilize equipment more productively. These are initiatives that may be HR in nature, but directly impact the organization's strategic goals. These types of action taken on your part are the initiatives that will elevate your position in the organization to one of an executive level member of the team.

Be your own cheerleader

It's not enough for you to know the strategic initiatives you have on your plate. Others don't know your focus has changed – they just want another ID card for dental insurance! You must publicize  new initiatives within the organization to provide context for the changes you are making in your role. You need to make a conscious effort to educate others in your organization that your priorities have changed. One simple way of doing this is to display your key goals for the year in your office for all to see.

In most organizations, when you walk into the VP of Sales office there is a large chart of sales for the month, top customers and top prospects. Enter the office of your Operations Manager and you are likely to see the critical jobs that need to be completed this week, equipment expected for installation and other leading indicators to meeting their goals. You should have the same chart in HR with your top initiatives for the year and your projects for implementation visible for all to see. These two sections are critical to show the focus on big picture issues. This will create a level of accountability between you and the leadership team, at the same time highlighting to employees that your focus is on overall corporate strategy and not getting them their lost paycheck stub!

Status Quo won't work

Once you have determined the action items that are a high priority for strategic HR, create a system of constant evaluation.

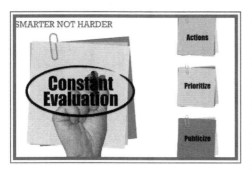

A task that is right today may not fit the organization in 2 years. Take time on a regular basis to step back and reevaluate your own processes. Expect your team to be constantly evolving and creating new ways of doing old tasks. Do not allow your HR team to fall into the common excuse of "that's the way we always did it." The world is changing too quickly to assume the ways of the past will forge a productive environment for the future without constant reassessment.

Taking responsibility for the fact that the administration of HR must be completed doesn't mean that you keep doing things the way they have always been done. The world of business is changing fast, and HR must evolve the same way. When was the last time you reviewed the capabilities of your payroll or HRIS system for functionality? It is common that we find organizations paying for the full suite of services from a vendor but only using a small fraction of what can be provided. Everyone attends systems training the week before a new computer installation, but who remembers all the functions that were introduced? It is common for standard reports to exist within your system that your team doesn't even remember are available. And is it possible that you purchased training the first year – and have been paying for it ever since?

But the work still needs to get done. Those three things on your original list may be important to employees or compliance regulations that can't be ignored. Consider looking to the services offered by your current vendors if you are still bogged down in administration. Aligning yourself with strategic partners that can add value and take routine tasks off your plate is often an effective strategy for human resources. Your payroll company, for example, should be sending check stubs signed and stuffed – ready to distribute. Or better yet, eliminate the option of check stubs and move to an online retrieval format for the few employees who care to look at their payroll information. During open enrollment, set the expectation that your benefit broker will bring all open enrollment documents copied and ready to distribute. If you have partners who expect you to be the administrator of their work – find new vendors!

It takes a village

Vendor management is an action step that can be considered critical in your role as a leader. Only by effectively managing vendors are leaders able to ensure that full value is received from the outsourced relationship.

While reviewing agreements and checking invoices can seem administrative, vendor management is actually a critical executive level action that supports overall strategy. There are four steps to vendor management that you should engage in with all vendors of the human resources department.

◀ - - - Understand their capabilities - - - ▶

Be sure you know what you are signing up for, what you have currently, and what you did not purchase at the original time of agreement. There may be services you needed initially that are no longer utilized. You may also want to add additional functionality later when you are comfortable with the new vendor and systems. Constantly evaluate your needs and vendor capability for ongoing alignment.

◀ - - - Set expectations - - - ▶

Have deadlines and quality thresholds that are acceptable to both parties. Everyone makes a mistake or two, but when will the vendor have crossed a line that you just can't tolerate? At the same time, understand what is expected from your team to be sure the vendor can accomplish their tasks. Create a system of notification if either side is not providing what is needed so you can fix minor problems before they become larger issues. Is your vendor willing to provide service level agreements to ensure they meet expectations? These will often provide a reduction in or rebated fees if you do not get the service that was promised in the agreement. You won't get these guarantees if you don't ask!

← - - - Annual review - - - →

Schedule a meeting annually with the sales representative and your daily contact at each vendor. During this meeting review the current agreement and discuss your level of satisfaction with the product or services. Ask about new initiatives the vendor is offering that you might be interested in. Be sure to ask if your team is providing what the vendor needs to give you the level of service you expect. How can you all work together to create an even better relationship in the new contract year? And certainly ask about fees or additional services. As you work with a vendor for extended periods of time, their job becomes easier. They know your players, have established systems, and will need to provide less training. This should be worth something in an ongoing relationship.

Conduct a full review of the
← - - - marketplace every 3 years - - - →

This process is commonly called "Request for Proposals" or RFPs. Analyze what the competition has to offer every 3 years. The idea is not necessarily to switch vendors, but rather to learn what other companies are offering and how their price point compares to what you are paying. You may find a service which fills a void in your process  that your current vendor can provide. Your current vendor may have assumed you weren't interested or the offer came across in an email that you quickly deleted! Allow your current vendor to present their services as if you were a new prospect as well. By hearing their typical sales presentation you may learn about a new product or service that would work well within your organization. It is also helpful if they understand that you are going through this process and your business is not necessarily theirs forever!

Consider the vendors with whom you are working today. Which ones have you not reviewed for some time? Call one vendor in the next month and review their services. Use the table below to see if there are efficiencies to be gained or service levels to be clarified.

	Current Vendor	Competitor #1	Competitor #2
Capabilities utilized and required			
Capabilities desired if available			
Deliverables required – service and time frame			
Service team			
Communication style			
Ability to have in-person meetings			
Billing cycle – payment and financing options			
Cost of total deliverables			

Data drives commitment and results

Whether we like it or not, data drives business. Change is determind by new data and is an inevitable part of long-term success. CEOs count on concrete numbers to make decisions that involve risk and all business decisions involve risk. Understanding and being able to articulate your initiatives in terms of ROI and cost of capital will solidify your argument for the next proposal you bring to the leadership team. As the top HR person, numbers and data can be critical as you propel your career. If you can't get your head around data gathering and analysis, get an HRIS that is easy for you to gather and report relevant data.

CEOs have an expectation of actionable data from sales, marketing, and production, and it should be no different for HR. If you want to play in the executive sandbox, you have to be prepared with data that will help you create action plans that predict future success. You must be ready to create action plans for change and then be held accountable for those results. This takes work, and possibly a set of skills and/or competencies you may not possess today. Learning these skills and the new vocabulary of business is not difficult. It is an important component of being an executive.

Don't just start creating reports and sending data around the company. You must be providing and relying on data that your leadership team finds useful.

Let's look at recruiting and common data that HR provides. There is little significance to executives when you bring up time to hire or turnover rate without context of how that impacts the business. Executives might find the facts you provide interesting, but they can't use the information to make decisions. Rather, consider sharing common skill sets of successful recent hires and then show how HR will create programs to find and capitalize on this talent. Your solutions may include a new recruiting tool or pre-employment testing. This would tell executives that while you may be taking additional time to fill positions, the new team members are becoming productive more quickly and the retention rate is higher. The action plan you create should focus on getting the right people in the right seats more quickly which will reduce overtime, increase quality, and provide internal clients a quicker turnaround. These are the issues that drive the business. Use your HR expertise to generate data that can solve a critical business issue, and you will quickly be have a SEAT at the management table on a regular basis.

Oh, and those custom reports! How many hours do you or your team spend pulling data, creating charts and spreadsheets, and sending them to various departments in your organization? Talk to managers about whether or not the reports HR is  creating provide them with the additional information they need to make decisions. Try omitting one or two, and see if anyone notices the report is missing. They may just be getting the email and saving it – without taking any action on the information. If so, it is a waste of your time to run the report, even electronically. Consider providing an overview sheet of highlights you see within the report - rather than providing the whole report. If you don't see anything of business interest, have a conversation with management regarding the decisions they make that utilize the data in the report. Understand why they find the information useful, and how you might be able to provide even more value with less effort. This conversation will have the added advantage of elevating your position from one of data deliverer to data analyst and contributor for the organization.

Create reports and provide data that will support the strategic goals of your organization. Don't provide your CEO with all sorts of statistics that show your team is doing its job. Create three to five meaningful data points that will point leaders in the direction they are working to drive the business. For instance, instead of time-to-fill a position in recruiting, create a correlation between recruiting sources and performance review scores in the first 90 days. That is meaningful information that you can use to bring better talent into the organization. Everything you measure for your team will drive its performance. The time-to-fill metric will create an incentive for your department to put a body in the seat, and this is likely not the appropriate long-term goal. Rather, consider a metric that would reference the HR team member coordinating recruiting with the score of the new hire on your 90-day review. Successful placements should be those new hires who are successfully integrated into their positions and receiving a good review from their managers after a 90 day period.

Invite yourself

How do you take strategic action if you aren't at the leadership table today? If you are not currently involved in the management team or strategic planning process, start with internal business partners that are on the management committee with whom you feel you have a good rapport. Approach them and ask which portions of the strategic plan they are working on this year. Ask how they see HR fitting into that goal. Press for ways you can add value by training talent, identifying new resources in the community, restructuring teams etc. Meet with each member of your management team and find at least one new goal human resources can work on to support the overall corporate strategic plan.

Then...set up a meeting with the CEO. Let the CEO know that you have evaluated the strategic plan and have ideas as to how HR can help. Lay out your goals in a SMART (Strategic, Measurable, Action oriented, Realistic and Timely) way. When you talk to the CEO, be sure you are giving a high-level overview of your ideas while still being specific about how the action will impact the organizational effectiveness. Use precise business language outlining what the total cost will be. These are the two factors that your CEO will be focused on. Your agenda in this meeting is for the CEO to see you taking action, looking at the big picture, and adding value to the bottom line. Don't get hung up on whether they like every idea – the objective of the meeting is to show value. Walk away with one or two new action items that will begin to show the CEO why you deserve a SEAT at the Table.

Influence and credibility builds authority

As an executive, you have to work to build credibility and influence within the organization. By integrating with all the departments and leaders in your organization, you will have a broad understanding of the entire organization. These components, when handled professionally and with clear action will provide the level of authority that you are looking for in your personal career development. Be sure that you are using this authority to the best interest of the organization, keeping the needs of your internal constituents in mind.

People don't have time to come to a meeting or read an email because you think they should know something. Every touch point with employees should be seen as an opportunity to continue to embrace the organizational mission. For instance, can you use open enrollment as a time to communicate company performance? Is your performance review process aligned with the characteristics of long term successful team members and the strategic plan? Does your employee engagement survey provide opportunities for organizational wins, or just a forum for employees to vent? If there is not a purpose to your action that is consistent with the strategic goals of the organization, consider whether or not the activity adds value.

A perfect example is the performance management process. It is commonly discussed at all levels of management that performance review processes are a waste of time and don't provide any value. In most organizations, the annual performance review is akin to the weather report we all rely on daily. We kind of have to check it – but it's often wrong and at the end of the day really doesn't provide a lot of value. Where else do we see consistent failure and disdain tolerated? When asked, executives are often disappointed about the lack of productive information that is generated during the annual performance reviews. Use this forum as an opportunity to take action and show the leadership team that you understand the value of time and money. HR initiatives that do not drive success will not be tolerated. Create a performance review program that will deliver results and be aligned with the organizational goals while still meeting the feedback and compliance needs you know exist.

Think outside the box when creating action items. An interesting initiative that might meet the needs of both the organization and employees is flexible work scheduling. If this is something your employees want, don't go to the management committee with the idea that it will help in recruiting and raise engagement scores; rather, talk about the ability to reduce office space, operate in inclement weather and serve customers more hours each day using employees in diverse regions. At the same time, educate employees that surveys continually cite the need for socialization in the workplace, so permanent tele-commuting is not realistic for the whole organization either. These are arguments that are substantiated by data that will be meaningful to managers and employees alike. The argument should be that moving to flextime and some amount of telecommuting will drive sales and reduce overhead. At the same time it will allow for retention of top talent. This is the kind of action the leadership team expects from its HR executive.

Define your team

Teams in human resources come in all shapes and sizes. It is common that there is a single HR professional, and often that person is handling a variety of other office management and accounting functions. Sometimes it's a line manager who has their mind on running the business and HR is an afterthought. And for some, HR is a full department with all levels of our pyramid covered by various individuals. Whatever the HR function looks like in your organization, the structure of how you handle the function is critical.

Your HR team needs to understand that their function is about creating actions and being accountable to the organizational attainment of strategic goals at the end of the year. You must be clear with your team members that they will be held accountable to focus their efforts on the activities that drive strategic results. Human resources has a tremendous impact on strategic goals by hiring the right people, ensuring they are trained properly, and having the tools to handle administrative issues without effort during the workday. Being an HR leader requires you to keep the focus of your team on these activities.

For the majority of HR departments, this is a new way of operating. We are all appreciative of the need to serve internal customers with the highest level of professional service. At the same time, we have a greater need to ensure that the organization is sustainable in the future in order to provide a workplace of choice for our employees. This should be the primary focus of human resources. As long as you and the management team are aligned in your goals and deliverables, you will have success.

> **Be an ACTION-oriented and accountable partner to your leadership team as your third step to taking that SEAT at the table.**

Chapter 6 — Technology

> Technology is nothing. What's important is that you have a faith in people, that they're basically good and smart, and if you give them tools, they'll do wonderful things with them.

Steve Jobs, Founder Apple

The HR executive of today must be entrenched in the latest technology and evaluating how it can be utilized to meet organizational profitability. So why do so many HR people still resist the technological advances we see in accounting, operations, and marketing? Technology can help you process a great deal of HR work today, yet HR is typically far behind the rest of the organization in its implementation.

Technology is the wave of the present and the future and must be supported by the HR function. Implementing technology in any area of the organization can be a daunting task but one that typically pays for itself in the end. HR technology should be used, at a minimum, in your organization as a part of the payroll and/or benefit function. The ability to maintain programs and data "in the cloud" can often make the implementation of human resource software much easier, frequently as simple as turning on a switch. The short-term effort of implementation should never trump the long-term benefit of moving to a technological solution for administrative tasks.

In most organizations, technology should be used for payroll, employee files, benefit administration, and performance management at the most basic level. HR leaders often say, "we are too small for technology" or "there is no room in our budget." There are systems that enhance the automation of all aspects of HR which are available in sizes and shapes that fit all organizations. Incorporating technology may run the spectrum from using Excel spreadsheets to robust human resources information systems. They should be utilized in a way that fits the organizational culture, budget, and administrative needs. Anything that reduces the time spent on administration and increases the data quality provided to leadership is a positive step forward.

They can get it done

HR departments constantly insist that they cannot trust people to mange HR programs and input data themselves. HR Managers love to cry:

"Employees will never be able to enter a new address, change a benefit level, or enter time properly into the systems. It will take me twice as long to clean it up then if I just do it myself."

HR administrator

If that were the case, they would have been fired a long time ago! The truth is these employees are using ATMs, smartphones, and email on a regular basis. If employees cannot figure out how to get through an open enrollment process online, should they really be trusted to use the computer-driven equipment in operations or the accounting system they need every day to input charges to your customers? If you think your system really is too complicated for your employees, consider a new system!

Of course, there may be a few within your organization that may not have the ability to handle technology. Solutions can, and should, be created to meet the needs of this small group. Don't fall into a trap that would negate technology for the masses to accommodate the exceptions necessary for a few. HR has a reputation of always seeing what can't be done and telling managers what they can't do. As a group, we have to overcome this perception and be problem solvers for the business, just as is expected from every other functional area.

Create a 24/7 service model

Embrace technology as a way to increase the efficiencies of your department and improve the experience for your internal customers. Managers want to pull data and run reports from anywhere in the country. Employees want benefit questions answered at 3 a.m. Applicants want to know the status of their application without bothering the recruiter. A simple human resources information system can make all of this happen with little ongoing effort by the HR department. The implementation may take some time, but the long-term advantages of resources that are available around the clock for meaningful strategic project management is enormous.

As with any change, there will be pushback from users and glitches in the initial phases of the project. Implementation of a new software is never fun, and no one ever thinks they have enough time to get it done. It may mean some late nights and weekends, that are available around the clock for your internal customers is enormous. And you benefit by adding time for strategic project management. Get buy-in from the rest of the leadership team and expect them to support the new system. The long-term advantage of implementation is that you will have a function that can run 24/7 and your involvement in administration will be greatly reduced. Knowing that after implementation you'll be able to focus on meaningful projects and create an HR organization that you are proud to lead is the home run you can expect when you hit the project out of the park.

Where to begin

Consider that a number of HR vendors include productivity improving technology with their products, many of which are included in the price you are already paying.

Examples might be:

- ☞   Payroll system – Virtual files and performance management

- ☞   Benefit Vendors – Open enrollment portal and benefit communications

- ☞   Job Posting sites – Applicant tracking and integration of hired candidates with payroll systems; Candidate report generation

Understanding these capabilities is a critical part of the vendor management we discussed earlier. Using current capabilities of the software, you may be able to implement relevant time saving technology into your team with minimal expense to the organization. However, just because you install it doesn't mean it will get used!

We see many organizations with the ability to use electronic employee files still insist on filing paper copies. The same paper pushing goes on in benefit administration, payroll information updates, performance management, and more. These activities can all be done electronically and reduce the need for the HR team to handle paper. When asking HR administrators why they don't rely on technology, they insist that having a back up is critical and the work has to be checked manually. This is simply a way to create work for people and must be stopped. Talk to your vendors and see what is available today that you can implement without learning new systems or making dramatic changes. Then set the technology ship in motion and insist your team jump aboard or be left behind.

Connections through customer service

HR will always be responsible for guiding employees through every transaction in the employment life cycle. Your HR department puts a high value on customer service and is fearful that will be lost in a move toward technology. Look for other opportunities for your HR team to create touch points and stay personally connected with the employee population. New hire orientation should focus on creating a link with corporate culture – not completing paperwork. Performance management should be about a two way conversation focused on the future, not just finishing the form to get it into the file. These are examples of situations where we can embrace technology for document management, and utilize our teams for meaningful interpersonal dialog.

Of course there are times we are still required to process paperwork, but this should be seen as a training opportunity for entry-level staff. Create opportunities where processing and administration can help a new HR team member understand what the computer has to do and appreciate what to look for when it goes wrong. If there is something being done that does not require critical evaluation or does not provide a learning opportunity, find a computer to do it!

Your employees are familiar with services moving to technology such as online banking, self-checkout lines at the grocery store, and shopping on Amazon. The change will be no different with the human resources function. The HR staff will still be the point person for issues and be available to assist employees who are struggling with the new systems. For example, if an employee loses an insurance ID card, does your HR department take care of getting the employee a new one? The employee should be encouraged to call the carrier and get a card or just print a card off the carrier website. You want your HR team to be available for the employee that has just received a life altering medical diagnosis and needs to understand how to navigate benefits for world-class care. That is providing customer service that supports the long-term strategy of HR and your organization.

You might say helping with an ID card is not a big deal, and you like the interaction with the employee. Consider that it will take fifteen to twenty minutes and stop your team member from whatever work is being completed at the time. There is likely to be the additional visit from the employee when the card does not arrive

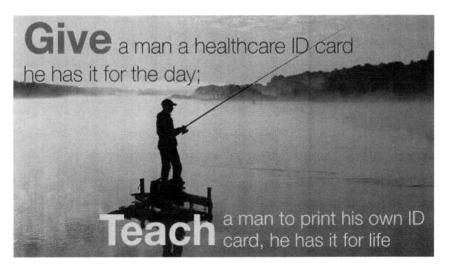

Give a man a healthcare ID card he has it for the day; Teach a man to print his own ID card, he has it for life

quickly enough, a name is misspelled, or other ongoing issues arise. The same transaction can be accomplished through technology that will enhance turnaround time as well as accuracy for most of the administrative HR tasks. If you want an HR department that drives organizational success, empower employees with self-service technology to meet their needs as often as possible.

> **As digital equipment replaces the jobs of routine works and lower-level professions, technicians are needed to install, monitor, repair, test and upgrade all the equipment.**

– Robert Reich, Former US Secretary of Labor

Human capital will always be a critical component of all organizations. Even as technology continues to evolve, we will need employees. Technology might have the advantage of not calling in sick or having productivity issues, but it does break down and enhancements seem to be never ending. As former Secretary of Labor said above – we just need different types of employees to meet the technology demands of the future definition of work.

Who is going to pay for it?

Technology implementation generally costs money. It's your job to convince the CEO why this investment will be good for the top or bottom line. When asking for funding, show the Return On Investment (ROI) and provide deliverables that you will be accountable for achieving. Your  organization approves expenditures in marketing, operations, and finance; they will for HR too! But it won't ever be approved if you don't ask. Look at how leaders in other functional areas have presented a case to gain approval for their proposals. Ask for help developing your request and feedback on your presentation. Don't be afraid to ask vendors for success stories, spreadsheets, and other supporting documents that will help make your case. Providing relevant data, actionable deliverables, and realistic goals for the program will help you gain executive level approval.

Technology in HR should be an expected solution to process enhancement, as it will reduce costs and free up time to focus on the organization's strategic needs. While there may be a capital investment, keep in mind that technology doesn't get sick and your data capture will be of higher quality than having entry-level employees input the information by hand.

Utilizing technology in the human resources function can reduce the need for human resources administrative staff as well as allow the HR team to focus on higher-level strategic activities. Embracing technology in the HR function shifts the employee population away from relying on HR staff to meet their every need. Instead, we provide an human resources function that is creating meaningful career paths, the providing training for development, and considering pay and benefit models that meet employee needs. Now that's the definition of human resources most leaders want to be a part of.

And then the law comes into play

Compliance issues relating to technology cannot be ignored. Once we allow employees to be more self-sufficient and access our systems, we must be cautious that our data is not compromised and security is not breached. The world of technology compliance is evolving in all aspects of business. As technology impacts human resources, critical compliance issues surround the ownership and privacy of data. Working with your IT leader is critical as you evaluate the interaction between employees and systems.

Common intersections of HR and IT are being explored by HR departments on a regular basis. Ensure that you have a close relationship with your IT counterpart and they are willing, interested, and available to help evaluate new policies as technology continues to evolve. The most common issues we are facing today include:

← - - - Internet access - - - →

Employees are regularly given access to the Internet. The company should monitor this access and have a written policy that covers sharing of data and downloading programs onto company systems. Most importantly consideration must be given to blocking access to sites that are not appropriate. We all know about the sexually explicit sites, but do your employees have access to Monster, Career Builder or other job search sites during the work day? If so, these are the first few sites I would block!

← - - - Viewing employee communication - - - →

Employees still seem to have a notion that when they use our systems for private communication there is an expectation of privacy. Recent policy indicates that employee's should be notified whether their email and Internet use will be tracked and/or viewed by the company. Include this policy in the employee handbook or a separate information technology policy. Be sure that your IT teams understand what information you will need to be able to view. Generally we only look at employee communication when an issue arises. Backups are common, but those files can be difficult to access if you are looking for limited data from one employee. Communicate the expectation to your IT team that you might need to look at one employee's history at any point in time.

← - - - Bring Your Own Device (BYOD) - - - →

This policy will establish the relationship between your employee's smart phone, tablet (or latest device!) and your organization. Employees commonly use their own devices to connect to organizational resources. The complexity of this has risen as a hot topic yet it continues to be an area that most groups have ignored. Organizations are analyzing the cost of providing smart phones to employees with the loss of control of data security. Most major organizations are creating, defining, and implementing BYOD policies to address common issues with technology security.

◆ – – – Security – – – ➤

Passwords protect unauthorized use of programs and data, but employees typically find passwords cumbersome. Their solution is often to have a list of passwords pinned to the cubicle wall, or post it notes displayed all over the monitor. Your organization must have policies about security. What is the appropriate method of password storage, and how are those shared in your organization? How will you gain access to resources if an employee terminates without providing passwords for key programs? This should be discussed and communicated to employees.

> **Social Media is a bullet train...and it isn't coming home anytime soon"**

Howard Schultz, CEO Starbucks

◆ – – – Social media – – – ➤

The concept of protected concerted activity requires you to allow an employee to voice their opinion about working conditions to a group of other employees. In the 21st Century this may be via facebook or twitter. At the same time there is awareness that employee conversations have never been so accessible to the entire world. To help employers navigate the protection in a world of global communication, the National Labor Relations Board provided guidance in 2012 regarding employee policies on social media. All organizations should be familiar with this recommendation and adopt a similar policy. While it is difficult to regulate employee communication, you can set expectations about the privacy of your processes, clients and other employees.

So remember.......

Aligning your human resources operation with a skilled technology administrator is an important connection for your department. Consider the compliance issues of retaining applicant data, storage of emails for use in employment law cases, and monitoring employee communication for investigation of workplace issues. It may not occur to HR to have these conversations with IT to ensure that the information is being stored as you anticipate. You should have a regular update with IT to make certain that data retention policies are in line with the actual practices of their function. Where you have a dedicated technology team for your operation, it is essential that they work closely with HR in these situations. If you do not have a dedicated IT team, spend time with the IT vendor to ensure your data is secure and retained.

Many smaller organizations utilize their payroll vendor as the primary go-to resource for HR technology and information retention. Larger organizations may have a stand-alone Human Resource Information System they utilize for documentation and reporting. HR and IT should work together to select vendors and manage agreements for any of these products. Standards will need to be set that spell out IT configurations and responsibilities as well as the requirements of the HR team. When the system is down, you want the alignment with your IT function to ensure everyone is working together to get your resources back on line as soon as possible.

Embracing technology is an effective way to show you deserve a SEAT at the table. You will demonstrate your ability to be an executive with forward thinking, new ideas, be accountable to initiatives, and strategic in your alignment with the rest of the organization. All leaders are pushing their teams to utilize technology to advance departments and reduce the size of staff required for administration. Use this as an opportunity to embrace this new way of doing work as an HR executive.

> **Be a TECHNOLOGY oriented partner to your leadership team as your fourth step to taking your SEAT at the table.**

Take control of your career

Chapter 7

> The biggest rival I had in my career was me. I couldn't control Arnold Palmer, Gary Player, Tom Watson or Lee Trevino. The only person I could control was me.

Jack Nicklaus, Professional Golfer

Literature on the topic of HR leadership consistently highlights the common competencies of an HR executive as:

- Trusted advisor
- Executive
- Business Minded
- Innovator
- Vendor Manager

These are the characteristics that your business needs and you must embrace to move your career forward. However, you can't expect that managers who have seen HR as an administrative support function for their entire career will suddenly embrace HR as a leadership position. It is up to the CEO and HR to work together to generate the respect and trust the whole organization can embrace and understand. As with all leaders, trust must be earned, so it is up to you to find opportunities to demonstrate these competencies to your leadership team. HR must be accountable for driving visible goals and action items that move the business toward their strategic goals.

> **Be a Strategic Executive who takes Action and embraces Technology**

HR agenda items should be given equal attention at management meetings, as they are critical to the mission of all organizations. All managers should be expected to respect human resources as the critical driver of an organization's success. As the HR leader, you must present new ideas and initiatives in a way that justifies both the expense and reward for the organization. Bring the overall impact of the situation you are discussing to the management team in a way they understand, focusing on how your plans will support the long-term strategic goals of the organization. HR executives should be expected to make compelling arguments supported by data; managers will listen when they see the alignment with the strategic plan supported by critical business oriented thinking.

Evaluate your HR tasks critically. Don't be afraid to outsource pieces of HR responsibilities that are transactional and provide little value to your strategic goals. Outsourcing can be a key strategic initiative that is aligned with your organization's profitability structure. Embrace technology in all aspects of the employee life cycle and set the expectation with employees for ongoing use. New initiatives should be delivered in a way which will improve quality and communication as well as ensure employees have access to critical HR information 24/7.

Control your own destiny

By now you have determined the direction in which you want to take your HR career and what changes you need to make to reach your goal. That may mean that you have made changes in your personal outlook or changed the focus of the HR department within your organization. Or – you may have decided that you don't want a *SEAT at the table* and are happy with a career that is focused on other parts of the HR pyramid. You may savor the HR generalist role that is focused on customer service. You may determine that being a subject matter expert in one of the functional areas of HR is the right career path for you. Handling the administrative aspects of HR can be quite rewarding and continues to be a necessary part of the HR function. These all lead to career aspirations that are those you find exciting to pursue. Be your own champion and follow the career path that is right for you.

Align with your CEO

Whatever your desired outcome, it is imperative that your CEO agrees on what is needed from HR to move forward within your organization. You want to be forthcoming with your goals and gain agreement from the CEO that this fits the direction of the organization. If not, determine the best way to meet the human resource needs of the organization and still have the career that you aspire to have.

As a starting point for your new HR initiatives we sum up a number of action items, which can be an effective springboard for HR success. We hear CEOs as a group discussing the competencies below as what they envision as drivers for future business. HR executives can be a valuable part of the successful equation in leadership teams by embracing these actions.

◀ − − − Be a proactive business leader − − − ▶

HR often sees the forest through the trees given their strategic position as an outsider in many departments but a team member who is still inside the organization. You should feel comfortable elevating any situation within the organization or external community that impacts your organization. Raise the conversation with a possible solution or two to leaders proactively. HR must understand what is happening in the internal and external environment at all times to be able to start these discussions at all levels of management. The human resources function should be counted on to create initiatives that will address the business needs long before there is an issue. At the same time, organizational leadership must involve HR in everyday conversations so the knowledge of employee situations is through ongoing analysis and not crisis management.

Identify and focus on your top and
← - - - high potential performers - - - →

Know who are the top performers in the organization today and who will be driving success in the future. Lead the management team through this evaluation and then create programs that will enhance the skills and ensure retention of this critical group. That doesn't mean treating all employees the same. Managers are

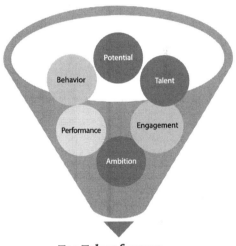

Top Talent for your organization

tired of hearing, "if we did it for Steve we have to do it for Jane." Every situation is different, and HR has to be open to helping find a workable solution for the business. Yes, it is HR's job to be careful of discrimination, but at the same time, some employees deserve more flexibility than others. Listen to needs, consider compliance, and provide options. Have a solid business reason for differentiation and allow management to act on that.

Use best practices as a guide, but
← - - - create your own path - - - →

All executives should be participating in industry conferences as well as meetings that focus on their areas of expertise. You should attend HR events to stay current and learn about advancements in our careers. Be sure to bring this knowledge back to your organization and share changes in the world of work with your leadership team. You must take on the same level of learning with the industry developments that impact your organization. All business people look forward to sharing information and best practices, but it's unrealistic to assume everything you hear will be a cookie cutter fit within your culture. You must evaluate new ideas, then use these practices as a launching pad for the innovation that will support the structure, culture, and goals of your organization. Best practices you learn should be used as a compass heading you in new direction - not a roadmap with specific turns that must be followed.

← - - - Understand total compensation - - - →

Total compensation is a buzzword in HR, but one that is not always embraced within organizations. A total compensation mindset is one that considers all aspects of your employee's life. This may be the fact that you allow casual dress – saving on purchasing a work wardrobe and dry cleaning. Do you offer work from home opportunities when needed, allowing employees to handle home repairs, for example, without taking time off work? Managing these programs takes time, communication, and documentation, but will often pay off exponentially in terms of recruiting and retention.

Top talent and identified high potential employees should be recognized and rewarded. If not rewarded properly, your key talent today and for the future will run, not walk, to the competitor. Pay for performance needs to be integrated into the culture of the organization and considered by the entire management team as a critical component of success. Be responsible for reminding managers to provide meaningful feedback and development opportunities to top talent. HR should be accountable for the implementation of a mindset of total compensation with leadership and create action-oriented communication across the organization.

Be the business person first

As the HR Executive, you must be the businessperson that adds value beyond the cost of the human resources function. It is incumbent on you to identify how the line items in your budget impact employees and take responsibility for the oversight of those items. HR should keep an eye on overtime and notify the proper manager if they are running outside the budget. If sales, quality and customer service are drivers in your organization, then your having employees ready and able to meet those demands are critical. Show the CEO and leadership team the value you can add by ensuring that the critical functions are staffed, evaluated, and trained to meet the demands of the organization. And then go one step further – watch and listen for other threats to the organization or opportunities for improvement and bring them to the leadership table before anyone else does!

You need to be the Human Resources executive that is going to be a trusted member of your executive team. Own the need for HR and find the right fit that meets the needs and culture of your organization for the future.

In the end, as an HR leader ensure your programs and initiatives demonstrate that you are a **Strategic**, **Executive** with **Actionable** plans that utilize **Technology**. With this in mind, you will create success and be the leader that you deserve to be and **take your SEAT at the table**

About the Author

Lori Kleiman is a human resources speaker, author, and consultant with more than 30 years of experience advising companies on HR issues. Her background gives her unique insight on how HR professionals and executives can work together effectively to achieve business goals. Lori Kleiman has consulted with nearly 450 organizations spanning a 30-year career in Human Resources. She grew up in a family-owned business, then went on to build – sell and create another company as an entrepreneur.

In 1998, Lori founded HRpartners, a boutique HR consulting firm that was acquired by Arthur J. Gallagher & Co. in 2007. Lori continued to work with Gallagher for six years to lead the firm's HR consulting practice before branching out again as an independent author, speaker, and consultant.

Mastermind Groups

PHR/SPHR Test Prep

Webinar Series

Weekly Blog

Books and toolkit

Today, Lori is a professional speaker and writer. Her Company - HR Topics is a resource for executives and human resources professionals to gain insights into the HR function. Through peer-to-peer advisory groups, consulting and training programs, Lori makes herself available to others to drive their success forward.

Lori has a master's degree in human resources, is a certified HR professional and is a member of the National Speakers Association. Through countless presentations Lori provides action-oriented solutions to common HR situations.

Sharing her love of HR with adult learners, Lori is an adjunct faculty member at at a number of Chicago area Universities and community colleges.

Bring Lori to your next event!
Customized programs are available for in house training, conferences and association events!

She splits her time between in Chicago, Illinois and Bonita Springs, Florida (guess which months she is where!) with her husband. Together they have three grown children.

Learn more at www.hrtopics.com

Lori's first book

HR departments cost money and spend the day telling managers what they can't do." We frequently hear this from CEOs of mid-sized firms. This was closely followed by, "HR is a necessary evil." How do executives know the value that HR can bring? Should HR have a limited, administrative function— or be outsourced altogether? Should it be expected to have a transformative role? Should it add value to the top and bottom line every day? Fire HR Now! is a thought provoking book for both CEO's and HR executives.

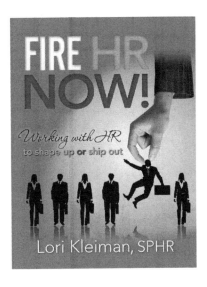

Fire HR Now! addresses the issues that cause CEOs the most pain, and provides HR executives a path for addressing those issues:

- ☞ Reflecting on what CEOs really want from HR

- ☞ Assessing HRs alignment with business goals

- ☞ Evaluating HR leaders capability of meeting corporate needs

- ☞ Taking action once they've decided on the best direction

Using a survey developed for the content of the book, CEO's and HR executives can have a constructive two way conversation leading to decisions of where HR is best aligned in your organization. We look at the needs of the organization and the skills of your HR team. At the same time, the book encourages HR leaders to evaluate if their career aspirations can be met in the current organization. After reading the book, both the CEO and HR leader will be able to take the next step to ensure HR is aligned with the organization. Lori delivers facts, tips, tricks and best practices in a way that appeals to executives: a bias toward actions that improve their operations right away, practical resources and tools to support progress, and a professional style with a dash of humor.

> Each chapter includes a special memo to HR to understand how to align with CEO's expectations

Lori's Second Book!

Here's the sad truth: most businesses have a self-defeating approach to human resources. We know this—and the other HR issues they face—because of our proprietary survey of nearly 450 companies, averaging 78 employees.

HR You can Use! provides answers to the 5 issues keeping business owners up at night.

HR You Can Use has a companion toolkit which provides all the forms, documents and web links that are referred to throughout the book.

   ☞   What should HR look like in my organization?

   ☞   How do you know if you're paying people properly?

   ☞   How do you successfully recruit the right employees?

   ☞   What can you do to keep good people?

   ☞   What laws do you need to be aware of, and how do you stay on top of them?

Organizations with fewer than 200 employees often don't require—or can't afford—an HR professional. That means they frequently parse out pieces of the function to several people. This can get them in trouble—from a process or compliance standpoint. And that lack of HR focus always keeps HR in a transactional rather than a transformational role. Executives never see the true meaning that would allow them to reduce their expenses while doing a better job running their companies.

To purchase the book and toolkit together visit www.hrtopics.com

Thank you for reading!

Dear Reader,

I hope you enjoyed *taking your **SEAT** at the table* and see how you can pull together the pieces of human resources for your own organization and career. Working with human resource professionals has always been my passion – and I am glad that we are now connected.

When I first came out with *taking your **SEAT** at the table* I received immediate feedback on how it helped take the mystique out moving your HR career up the corporate ladder – and allowed people to easily take a leadership role in their organizations. As an author, I love the feedback. I got some very constructive critiques that you will see incorporated in the text.

Candidly, you are the reason I am so passionate about this next professional journey. I want to help businesses and HR professionals grow – and I can only do that if I know what you are thinking – and needing from me. I'd love you to write me at lori@hrtopics.com with feedback – or visit my website at www.hrtopics.com to sign up for regular communication (*I promise – I won't send too much!*)

Finally, I need to ask a favor – if you are so inclined share your comments with others by writing a review on Amazon I'd appreciate your feedback on the book page. Love it, Hate it, Wish it was more – whatever your thoughts feedback helps us all grow!

I am happy to provide a FREE HR TOOLKIT to anyone who connects via the website, email or amazon!

Stay tuned as I continue to offer relevant HR content via webinar and new books!

Lori Kleiman, SPHR SHRM-SCP

Made in the USA
Middletown, DE
29 June 2015